Nature's Most Deadly?

Sean Callery

Character illustrations by Jonatronix

Contents

OXFORD
UNIVERSITY PRESS

Dangerously close?

If you meet danger, do you face it head on or take off faster than an Olympic sprinter?

It's an interesting question and one that has fascinated humankind for centuries. Throughout history, people have lived near animals that could kill them in a flash, from cavemen hunting mammoths to camera crews filming polar bears. Savage creatures feature in many of our stories; we seem fearful of them, yet drawn to the danger they pose.

In the past, fierce animals were often hunted or captured, and used for entertainment, forcing some species to the brink of extinction. Today many people are trying to save these creatures, but that's not the end of the story.

Can we live together?

We want to preserve these creatures but, with our growing population and demand for resources, humankind is getting alarmingly close to some deadly neighbours. Dangerous animals kill hundreds of people every year with victims being bitten by sharks, drowned by crocodiles, **mauled** by tigers, crushed by hippos and poisoned by spiders.

Is it possible to share our planet safely with dangerous beasts? Do animals have rights? Should we kill animals that pose a threat to humans? Do we have the right to change other animals' habitats? Is keeping dangerous animals in captivity right or wrong?

3

Right to FIGHT!

Would you want to watch fierce animals fight? What if one of the animals was a human? Such spectacles have been happening for thousands of years and continue to happen today. There's something about seeing danger up close that fascinates people.

Beastly battles

In the Roman era, spectators flocked to amphitheatres to witness men battle each other – gladiator against gladiator. But what if the opponent wasn't human? What if man fought beast? That's exactly what the **bestiarii** did. Armed only with a spear or a knife, they took on some of the world's most dangerous predators, fighting wild animals such as lions, panthers, bears and crocodiles.

11 000 animals were killed in 123 days during one Roman fighting festival in 107 AD.

DID YOU KNOW?

Roman prisoners, who had been condemned to death, were sometimes thrown, unarmed, into an arena full of hungry lions. They didn't stand a chance. One lion killed 200 men.

The bear pit

Bear-baiting was a popular 'sport' in Europe between the 12th and 19th centuries. Wild bears were caught and chained to a wooden stake in a bear pit – an open space with a fence around it to protect the crowd. Imagine the scene: ferocious dogs are led into the ring as the crowd places bets on whether the bear or the dogs will win.

Now imagine if the dogs were replaced by a *human*. Yes, like the bestiarii, it was sometimes knife-wielding humans who entered the bear pit to do battle.

Bear baiting was banned in Britain in 1835 under the Cruelty to Animals Act.

English diplomat Giles Fletcher sent this report from Russia in 1589.

"On other speciall recreation is the fight with wilde Beares, which are caught in pittes, or nets, and are kepte in barred cages... The man is turned into a circle walled round about, where he is to quite himselfe so well as he can, for there is no way to flie out. When the Beare is turned loose he commeth upon him with open mouth."

Is it right to make animals fight each other in the name of entertainment? Would *you* watch a person fight a lion or bear?

Cage RAGE

The 1975 film *Jaws* portrayed sharks as the ultimate scary monster of the sea. Actually, the image is wrong: left alone, most sharks won't attack humans (we are too bony for them!). But the 'monster' image stuck and our fascination with sharks now feeds the shark-tourism industry.

Bait called 'chum', a mix of fish parts and blood, is released into the water to draw sharks towards the cage, ensuring tourists get a thrilling face-to-teeth encounter.

tourists filming the experience

DID YOU KNOW?

There are about 400 species of shark but only a dozen of these have been known to attack people, the best known being the Great White.

Shark tourism: right or wrong?

Shark-diving is big business. About 600 000 people a year are lowered into the sea, protected by a metal cage, to experience the thrill of being within metres of these fearsome predators. But what impact does this have?

Positive impact

- People have the opportunity to appreciate beautiful sharks in their natural environment.
- Fewer sharks are killed for food if they are kept alive for tourism.
- Shark tourism supports 10 000 jobs in 29 countries.
- Sharks can't smell people through their wetsuits in bait-filled water, and they seem to see the cage as one big object, so the practice doesn't encourage them to think of humans as food.
- Sound vibrations can be used to attract sharks instead of 'chum'.

Negative impact

- It draws sharks far from their natural feeding areas, changing the balance of nature.
- Sharks get used to people and fear them less. This makes attacks on swimmers, surfers and divers more likely.
- The use of 'chum' means sharks associate people with food so they are more likely to come closer to people in the water and then more likely to attack.
- Sharks normally migrate but being fed bait encourages them to stay. What happens when people stop feeding them?
- Huge quantities of fish, and even small sharks, are killed to make the 'chum'.

Is shark tourism acceptable? Sharks are not physically harmed but are they harmed in other ways? Now you've read both sides of the argument, what do you think?

DID YOU KNOW?

Sharks kill about four people a year but humans kill at least 25 million sharks every year.

BIG business

Safaris have become a massive industry, attracting millions of tourists to countries such as Africa, where people pay big money to see some of the most spectacular animals on Earth.

Kenya's Masai Mara reserve, a popular location for safaris, had 6 lodges and about 300 beds in the 1980s. Today there are 25 lodges with ten times as many beds.

One in every twelve jobs in South Africa is in tourism and safaris are a major part of this.

Eco-tourism

Safaris bring much-needed money and jobs to an area. **Eco-tourism** helps to preserve the environment and to reduce poaching because tourists pay to see live animals in their natural habitats. However, the number of visitors can unsettle the animals, disrupting their feeding and breeding patterns. Extra traffic and new hotels also affect the environment, changing the animals' habitat.

DID YOU KNOW?

The main African safari countries are:

- Botswana
- Kenya
- Namibia
- South Africa
- Tanzania
- Zambia
- Zimbabwe

Safaris also take place in Brazil, Peru and Canada in the Americas; in Australia; and in Asian countries such as India, Indonesia, Bangladesh and Malaysia.

See Africa from every angle with Eco-Safari!

Go by bike, car, canoe, micro-lite, hot air balloon … or on one of our guided safaris.

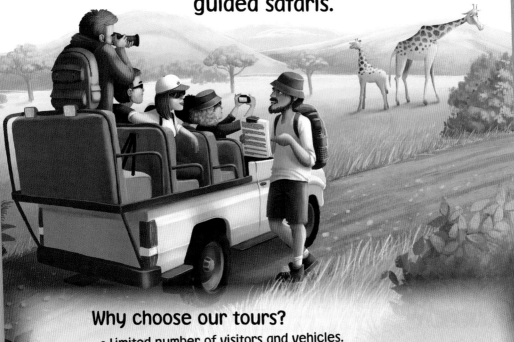

Why choose our tours?

- Limited number of visitors and vehicles.
- Guides who understand the animals and nature.
- Visitors take away their rubbish.
- Vehicles stay at least 20 metres from the animals.
- No one feeds or touches the animals.
- Profits from the safaris are used to help local people.

Would you go on safari? Do you think safaris harm the environment and animals, or does the money they provide help to preserve the animals?

In captivity

Zoos are not a new idea – they have existed for centuries. In Ancient Egypt, exotic animals were often brought back from expeditions as gifts for pharaohs.

Before television or the Internet, a visit to a zoo was the only way to see dangerous beasts such as lions, tigers and crocodiles. But do zoos have a place in the modern world?

Animal preservation

The experience of seeing animals up close makes them more real to people and so, it could be argued, helps people understand animals better. As a consequence, they may be more interested in protecting them.

> **There's still something extraordinarily exciting and appealing about that moment when you're standing at the edge of a zoo exhibit and that animal stares back at you.**
>
> Jeffrey Hyson, zoo historian.

Zoos also help to preserve endangered species, offering a safe environment, free from poachers and predators. They also act as a refuge for unwanted exotic pets and injured wildlife that would otherwise die.

In modern zoos, habitats resemble the animals' natural environments. In the past, animals were taken from the wild to populate zoos, whereas modern zoos run breeding programmes that aim to keep species from extinction and reintroduce them back into the wild.

The South China Tiger exists only in zoos; none live in the wild.

DID YOU KNOW?

There are 15 000–20 000 tigers in zoos around the world, five times as many as in the wild.

Unnatural habitats

Some people argue that zoos treat animals as possessions, denying them the right to live free. Zoo animals may live longer than wild animals but their quality of life can be reduced in captivity; they are not in their natural habitats and often don't have the same space to roam. They are also kept close to other species and human beings that they would not normally encounter in the wild.

> **Warehousing animals for life is not the way to save them from extinction. Their salvation lies in protecting habitats, not in creating animal prisons.**
>
> People for the Ethical Treatment of Animals, an animal rights campaign group.

Very few animals born in zoos ever return to the wild: they don't have the hunting skills or the knowledge of their habitat.

DID YOU KNOW?

Some zoo animals become bored and depressed and behave strangely, for example pacing repetitively. This is called **zoochosis**.

Do you think zoos have a place in the modern world? How far can a man-made environment mirror a natural environment?

Circus acts

For some people, seeing wild animals up close is not enough – they want to tame them too. Animal-taming has been a popular form of entertainment throughout history.

Taming lions to perform tricks, such as opening their mouths so a trainer could put their head inside, was a popular circus act for centuries.

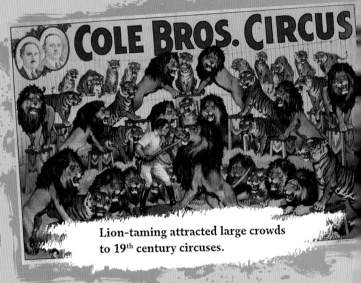

Lion-taming attracted large crowds to 19th century circuses.

Fearless first

In 1819, the first lion-tamer – Frenchman Henri Martin – adopted gentle horse-training methods in his work with tigers, based on encouragement and reward. American Isaac Van Amburgh took a tougher approach, however, using an iron bar to beat big cats to make them perform in his act in the 1830s.

Van Amburgh was the first man to put his head in a lion's mouth.

DID YOU KNOW?

Lion-tamers worked with a range of big cats that had usually been born and raised in zoos; the cats were not truly wild.

Cat woman

The world's first female tiger-tamer was American circus performer Mabel Stark. She performed in the 1920s in a cage containing 18 big cats. She was attacked so often in her long career that she sometimes did her act covered in bandages and walking with a cane!

Truly tamed?

Often these circus acts were not without their risks, with tamers suffering injuries, or even death. In 1872, a local newspaper, the *Sheffield Independent*, reported a fatal lion-taming performance.

DEATH OF MASSARTI, THE LION TAMER
HORRIBLE SCENE

A terrible scene occurred in Mander's Menagerie, Bolton, about half-past 10 o'clock on Wednesday night, January 3, Massarti, the lion tamer, being attacked by the lions…

…For a moment the spectators imagined it was part of the performance, but soon the agonized features of Massarti indicated that he was being attacked in reality. Immediately a scene of wild and terrible confusion ensued. Women screamed, and men ran for pitch forks, brooms, or any weapons they could lay their hand upon.

In the meantime, three other lions had lept upon Massarti…

The conflict was renewed again and again and several times Massarti was dragged up and down the cage, one lion seizing him by the head, the others by the legs….

A later examination of the body revealed frightful injuries.

Sheffied Independent,
January 1872

Acts with wild animals are banned in many countries but allowed in others. Do you think they should be allowed?

Killer thriller

Like a rocket from the water, a giant killer whale soars, its huge body curving as it crashes down, splashing the front rows of the laughing crowd.

Orcas have up to 56 curved teeth, designed for catching and ripping up prey.

This is a common sight for audiences in marine parks, who have paid for the chance to see these magnificent marine mammals close up.

But did you know killer whales are not really whales? They are actually large dolphins – their species name is orca. There are around 50 orcas in marine parks around the world, some captured from the oceans, others bred in captivity.

The question is: should they be there? Is it right to keep creatures, whose natural environment is the vast ocean, in marine parks for humans' entertainment?

Orcas in the oceans

Behaviour: Swim about 120 kilometres a day, hunting sea animals, cooling their bodies by swimming underwater.

Family: Orcas live in pods of 20-50 family members.

Communication: Orcas 'talk' with each other all the time and can hear sounds over many kilometres.

Diet: Fresh sea creatures, including fish and seals, from which they obtain water.

Lifespan: About 30-50 years.

Orcas in captivity

Behaviour: Swim in circles in large pools and are fed by humans. They spend more time on the surface and can overheat because of increased exposure to the sun.

Family: Kept alone or in a very small group.

Communication: Sounds bounce off the hard walls, confusing the orcas.

Diet: Frozen fish. This is dry, so they are also given water through a tube into the stomach.

Lifespan: Up to 20 years.

Drooping fin

Orcas in marine parks can develop a drooping fin, which rarely happens in the wild, and is thought by some to be a sign that the creatures are unwell.

However, others suggest it is a **genetic** feature of orcas bred in captivity.

Free Willy

The sad story of Keiko, the orca who starred in three films, shows how captured animals are sold on and how hard it is to reintroduce them into the wild.

Keiko's life story

1977	Born near Iceland.
1979	Captured and kept in an aquarium.
1982	Sold to a US marine park; started performing in shows.
1985	Sold to a Mexican marine park.
1993	Starred in three *Free Willy* films about a boy who befriends a killer whale.
1996	Moved to an aquarium in Newport, USA, to be trained for release into the wild.
1998	Taken to learn to fish off Iceland.
July 2002	Released into the open sea; failed to mix with other orcas.
October 2002	Lived in a **fjord** in Norway; fed by humans.
December 2003	Died aged 27.

Despite being trained to return to the wild, Keiko never settled back in the ocean.

Does the fun of seeing orcas perform make it OK to keep them in captivity?

Trophy pets

Fierce animals such as big cats, snakes and crocodiles are kept as pets around the world. But what's the appeal? Are they more desirable because they're unusual? Whatever the reason, many owners often don't know what they're getting into. Although exotic animals may be cute when they are young, as they grow bigger and stronger their natural instincts to hunt and kill become stronger too. Then the cute pet often becomes a threat.

As exotic pets mature and become larger and more unmanageable, it's not unusual for them to be given to zoos; their owners can simply no longer look after them. But what if the owners aren't responsible people and just release them into the wild?

There are up to 7000 pet tigers in the USA – more than in the wild.

Tragedy

On 5th August 2013, a 4 metre-long African rock python escaped from its cage above a pet shop in New Brunswick, Canada, and tragically strangled brothers Connor and Noah Barthe, aged six and four, who were sleeping nearby.

Living with danger

Animal	Adult characteristics	Dangers
Big cats (cougars, lions, tigers, leopards)	• Big, strong and territorial.	• Long, sharp claws for cutting and mauling. • Powerful jaws – they kill by biting or strangling.
Crocodiles and alligators	• Can grow up to 4 metres long.	• Powerful bites. • One whip of a tail can break a leg.
Snakes	• Grow very big – boa constrictors can grow 3 metres long. • Can become too fat if overfed. • Good at escaping.	• Some venomous snakes can kill adults • **Constrictors** can suffocate small children.
Primates (monkeys, chimpanzees, baboons, lemurs)	• Moody and unpredictable. • Very strong.	• Biting – can rip faces and chew off fingers. • Hitting. • Often carry diseases.
Bears	• Can grow to be enormous. • Unpredictable and likely to attack.	• Slashing with sharp claws. • Large canine teeth for biting and huge molars for crushing.

Would you want a dangerous pet? Should people be allowed to keep any pets they want?

Danger lurks

There is always a chance that captive animals might escape and, as with us, their first instinct is to find food to survive. That *could* mean hunting humans and so, when dangerous creatures escape, the police have to act fast. This is a true story from October 2011.

HOME   **NEWS**   COMMENTS   VIDEO   TECHNOLOGY

Police hunt escaped wild animals

Comment

US police officers went on a big game hunt when dozens of wild animals escaped from a sanctuary in Zanesville, Ohio. Forty-eight animals, including big cats and bears, were let loose by their owner, Terry Thompson.

The Sheriff's office received phone calls warning there were animals loose. The four armed deputies, sent to the animal sanctuary, found all the cage doors and fences open, and the wildlife hunt began.

As night fell, and there were still animals missing, it became too dangerous to try to tranquilize them in case they couldn't be found and then woke up, and escaped in the dark. The officers had no option but to shoot to kill.

Update

Comment

Sheriff Matt Lutz:
These are wild animals that you would see on TV in Africa. This is a bad situation.

Comment

Born Free USA:
It's a tragedy for these animals – for no fault of their own, they've been shot, and I can see how difficult that decision was for the police.

Update

Three leopards, a grizzly bear and two monkeys were captured and sent to nearby Columbus Zoo.

Update

The list of dead animals included 17 lions, 18 tigers, 8 bears, a wolf and a baboon.

Update

Mr Thompson had had many arguments with neighbours, who complained about noise and animals escaping from his property.

Should there be more **restrictions** on keeping exotic animals as pets?

Man's best friend?

Many people love the company and comfort of a pet dog. In fact, dogs are often called 'man's best friend'. But all dogs are descended from wolves, which are aggressive hunters, and certain breeds are considered so dangerous that they are banned in some countries and US states. Most commonly, these are dogs that were originally bred for hunting, such as the pit bull terrier.

Domestication of dogs

The history of the **domesticated** dog can be traced back to when humans hunted with wolves thousands of years ago. Wolves have sophisticated body language that they use for communication, which makes them highly successful hunters. When humans began hunting with wolves, it is thought that the partnership actually gave humans an advantage in the hunt and that led humans to domesticate them.

That's not to say, however, that dogs no longer have the traits of their ancestors. In fact, inherited behaviour, such as communication, may explain why dogs fit into human households so well today. However, it is thought by some that dogs, like wolves, also retain their natural predatory instinct and can be dangerous.

In this photo, one wolf is in trouble. It is in a passive position: on its back, paws drawn in to its body. The other wolves are displaying aggressive body language: teeth bared, fur bristled.

Dog attacks

In the UK, certain breeds of dog have been categorized as illegal because they are considered too dangerous to keep as pets. If a person is found to be keeping a dangerous dog, the owner is fined and the dog is **put down**. The law also states that it's illegal to sell, abandon, give away or breed from a banned dog.

But is that enough? Many other breeds of dog aren't on the list but are very powerful and could pose a real risk if provoked. The four breeds below are all illegal in the UK.

Pit bull terrier

Japanese Tosab

Dogo Argentino

Fila Braziliero

> " A dangerous dog can be any breed of dog no matter how big or small which isn't kept under control. "
>
> The Metropolitan Police Service, London.

DID YOU KNOW?

Between 2005 and 2012, 251 people were killed by dogs in America. Pit bulls and Rottweilers carried out 73 per cent of these attacks.

But is that enough? Many other breeds of dog aren't on the list but are very powerful and could be dangerous if provoked.

The SPORT of kings?

Famous prehistoric rock paintings in Tassili N'Ajjer, Algeria

The history of hunting goes back millennia, to a time when everyone had to hunt for their food. Early civilizations fed their families by **scavenging** – finding leftovers abandoned by top predators such as lions, leopards and tigers. However, when people learned to hunt animals such as deer and bison, predators such as wolves and big cats were competing against them for the same prey. The answer was for humans to kill the predators to protect the food supply.

Farming foes

The next time humans found themselves competing with predators was about 12 000 years ago when people started farming animals such as sheep and goats. These animals were easy prey so farmers found themselves once again hunting predators to keep their livestock safe.

Consequently, up until the Middle Ages the hunting of predators was mainly as a result of competition for food: humans killed animals to protect their food supply. After that the focus began to shift and hunting became a sport, particularly linked with wealthy people.

DID YOU KNOW?

In East Africa in 1909, a £50 license permitted hunters to kill: 2 buffalo, 2 hippos, 22 zebras, 84 monkeys, 281 antelopes … and any number of lions and leopards, because they ate cattle and were classed as vermin, like rats.

Big game hunting

The aim of big-game hunting was to track and kill one of the Big Five – lions, leopards, elephants, buffalo and rhinoceros. In the 19th century, as European countries expanded their empires into Africa and India, their hunters took what had once been a royal sport to a new level. Hunting became a sign of prestige – a test of wits and strength against a fearsome adversary.

Presidential prestige

One of the biggest hunting expeditions ever was led by Theodore Roosevelt soon after he left the US presidency in 1909. He and his son, Kermit, combined big-game hunting with collecting exhibits for the Smithsonian Museum, Washington, USA. They used 250 local guides and porters as they travelled by train, horse, camel and steamboat across Eastern Africa.

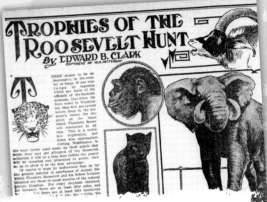

Theodore Roosevelt and his son returned with 23 141 specimens, including 5013 mammals.

The ex-president wrote to his sister Corinne in May 1909:

Big-game hunting is still allowed under strict controls. Would you go?

"I am sitting on a cool verandah with vines growing over the trellises, having just returned from a morning hunt in which I killed a python and an impala antelope. Yesterday I killed two antelopes, and the day before, a rhino and a hippo, and the day before that, Kermit killed a leopard which charged him viciously after mauling one of the beaters. I have also killed six lions – four of them big ones."

Nasty neighbours

The human population is growing and, as it does, we are **encroaching** into animals' habitats more and more – sometimes into the territories of some very dangerous creatures.

Perfect habitat

Florida is a US state with a rising population attracted by the warm climate and 18 000 kilometres of rivers, streams and waterways. This has also been the ideal habitat for American alligators for thousands of years. The result? Florida's 19.32 million people share living space with 1.3 million wild alligators!

Everglades City on the edge of the Everglades in Florida, USA

An alligator in a swimming pool in Tampa, Florida, USA.

> **People build their homes on lakes, canals and rivers, which is rightfully where alligators belong, so it should not be surprising that they show up where most people would rather not find them.**
>
> Kent Vliet, alligator expert at the University of Florida.

DID YOU KNOW?

Alligators have existed on Earth for the past 200 million years!

Avoiding the snappers

Alligators prefer smaller prey, so young children and pets are often targets, but even tall adults look small to an alligator from the water – no one is safe. Residents are advised:

- Never enter water at night, when the likelihood of attacks increases as alligators are nocturnal hunters.
- Never go near an alligator's nest – the females are fiercely defensive.
- Never feed alligators – they will associate humans with food.

Killer fangs

Australia's Sydney funnel web spider can kill people with its dangerous bites. So it's best to avoid it … which is hard when you build a city of 4.6 million people where it lives.

The spiders rest in cool, damp places during the day and they come out at night, sometimes falling into swimming pools where they can survive for up to 24 hours. When threatened, they repeatedly sink in their fangs, injecting powerful venom. Without treatment, victims can die within 15 minutes.

Are we to blame for animal attacks if we invade their habitats?

DID YOU KNOW?

Sydney funnel web spiders have killed 13 people including 7 children in the last 100 years. There have been no deaths from bites by this spider since 1981, after an antidote to its venom was developed.

Bear necessities

Do animals change their behaviour when they live among us? The town of Churchill in Manitoba, Canada, is on a migration route for polar bears that hunt seals on the frozen Hudson Bay in winter and return to land in the summer. The city has a long history with polar bears but in recent years the encounters have started to get frighteningly close! As the ice that allows the bears to get to their hunting grounds appears later and later in the year (many argue this is due to climate change), the bears look to other sources for food, including within the city.

A brief history of polar bears in Churchill, Manitoba

800 BC Nomadic Arctic people live in the region, hunting polar bears and other animals.

1943 A military base is established near the town. Servicemen shoot bears and ship the bodies home as trophies.

1717 AD A fur-trading post is built. Bears are killed for their hides and as food for sled dogs.

1969 The first patrol by the Polar Bear Alert Program is held to keep bears away.

1964 When the army base closes, the site becomes a huge rubbish dump, which attracts polar bears.

Churchill is called 'the polar bear capital of the world'.

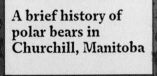

1981 The army base is demolished and a tourism industry based around viewing polar bears, birds and whales starts to grow.

1983 A man scavenging in a ruined hotel puts meat from its freezer in his pockets. The smell attracts a polar bear, which kills him.

2005 The town dump is closed.

2014 By now about 12000 people come to see the bears migrating each year.

1980 A 'polar bear prison' is set up to house bears that won't leave town.

Three-step plan

To manage the polar bear 'invasion' Manitoba Conservation has come up with a three-step polar bear programme:

1. Bears are encouraged to move on with noises such as car horns.

2. Those that stay are held in a 'polar bear prison' with air-conditioned cells, and released outside town when the bay ice is thick enough for them to hunt.

3. When the prison's 28 places are full, bears are captured and released 80 kilometres north of town.

The bears are air-lifted away from Churchill by helicopter.

What do you think of the way the people of Manitoba have adapted to living alongside polar bears?

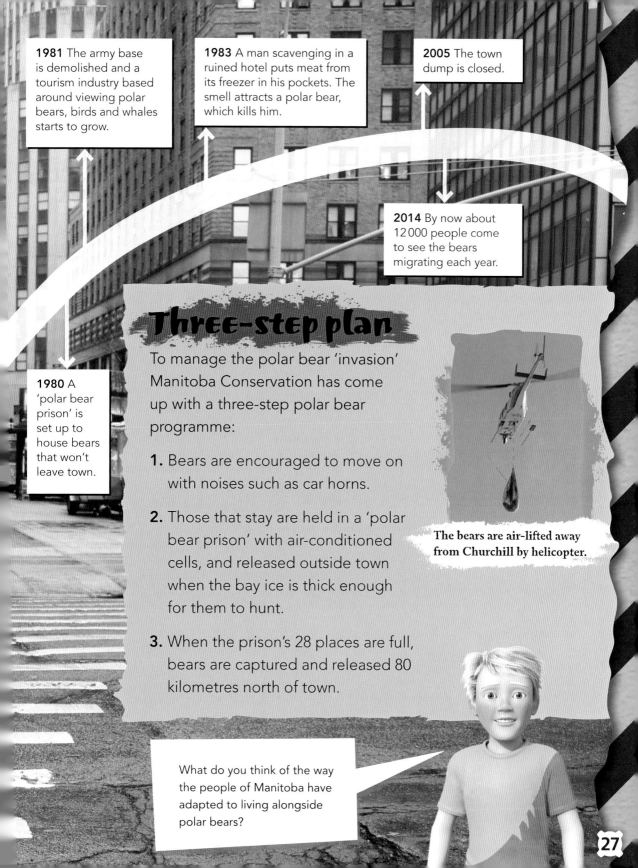

27

Culling controversy

If fierce animals become a threat, one option is to limit the population by **culling**. This is the process of reducing the number of animals by killing some of them.

The culling of dangerous animals has been considered in the following places:

- Wolves in Europe and Asia, because they are a threat to livestock.

- Crocodiles in Australia and Zimbabwe, because of the threat to people.

- Sharks in Australia, after a number of fatal attacks on swimmers.

- Pythons in the USA, where Florida is being overrun by released pet snakes that have bred.

These people are protesting against the culling of badgers. Badgers have been culled because they are believed to spread disease among cattle.

DID YOU KNOW?

Across the world, environmental campaigners have prevented many proposed culls. However, a python cull in Florida went ahead in 2013. In 30 days, 1600 hunters killed only 68 pythons out of an estimated 10 000.

An interview with an environmental campaigner

Journalist: The argument for culling is that it can be the most humane way to deal with a glut of animals, to redress the balance of nature so to speak. But you're against the use of culling, aren't you?

Campaigner: Yes, I am. I think nature has a way of doing this on its own, without interference from us. When one species dominates a food chain, it will run out of food. We, as humans, do not have the right to decide which wild animals live or die.

Journalist: But what do you say to the argument that if we don't kill these top predators then they will kill all the other wildlife; that culling could perhaps be the only way of getting rid of these dominant animals?

Campaigner: In nature, predators mainly kill the weak and injured, leaving the healthy wildlife to live and breed. If we do need to protect other animals or habitats from these dangerous animals, we don't have to resort to killing them. Noise devices and equipment such as fences and nets can deter them.

Journalist: But wouldn't those devices stop every animal rather than just the problematic ones?

Campaigner: Well, other non-violent ways of managing the population include raiding nests and removing eggs. This is what happens with crocodiles in Australia.

Journalist: I'm glad you've mentioned crocodiles. What do you say to the argument that we should cull animals, such as crocodiles, that endanger humans?

Campaigner: Crocodiles and other dangerous animals can't kill or harm us if we keep away from them. For example, instead of wading across a river, why not build a bridge over it? If we invade its territory, an animal will instinctively want to protect it.

What do you think? Should humans have the right to kill animals as a way of managing an animal population?

29

Fighting back

What happens when animals fight back against human invaders? The rhino, hippo and elephant are not carnivores but they *are* huge, powerful and territorial.

Ton of trouble

What is the most dangerous creature in Africa? A lion? It's actually the hippopotamus. This territorial beast will take on crocodiles and is said to kill more than a thousand people every year.

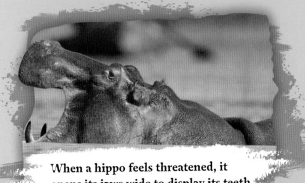

When a hippo feels threatened, it opens its jaws wide to display its teeth as a warning against attack.

Paul Templer was a tour guide leading a group by canoe on the Zambezi River in Zambezi in 1996 when a large bull hippo grabbed him.

Hippo attack

"I wriggled as hard as I could, and in the few seconds for which he opened his jaws, I managed to escape … but the hippo struck again, dragging me back under the surface … he clearly wanted me dead.

Hippos' mouths have huge tusks, slicing incisors and a bunch of smaller chewing teeth. It felt as if the bull was making full use of the whole lot as he mauled me – a doctor later counted almost 40 puncture wounds and bite marks on my body. The bull simply went berserk, throwing me into the air and catching me again, shaking me like a dog with a doll."

Big threat

Elephants are the world's largest land mammals and eat 270 kg of food a day. When they run out of vegetation, they raid farms, causing enormous damage, and when people try to move herds on they sometimes fight back. About 500 people are killed by elephants in Africa and Asia every year.

Elephants have no natural predators although lions will prey on the young. The main risk to these giant creatures is from poaching and changes to their habitat.

Rhino rage

As humans invade its natural habitat, the Asian rhino is forced to raid farmers' crops for food, bringing it into contact with people. The rhino can run at 48 kph and gore victims with its long, sharp horn. It kills about 100 people a year.

How can people safely share land with these creatures?

DID YOU KNOW?

Hippos kill more people each year than lions, elephants, leopards, buffaloes and rhinos combined.

Pack attack

If you get rid of dangerous animals, you get rid of the problem, right? Not necessarily. Killing the wolves in Yellowstone National Park, USA, changed the balance of nature and they were subsequently reintroduced. Follow the reasons that led to this decision and the different views as to whether this was the 'right' decision.

The history of wolves in Yellowstone National Park, USA

In the 1800s, American settlers slaughtered more than a million wolves.

The last wolf den in Yellowstone was destroyed in 1923. Over the following decades the herds of elk grew enormous and grazed more widely, including by streams.

This reduced the growth of willow.

Beavers had no willow branches to build lodges so the numbers of beaver ponds dropped.

This reduced the habitats of a wide range of other animals including insects, fish, amphibians, reptiles and birds.

DID YOU KNOW?

Some wild wolf packs have survived in France, Sweden and Norway. Ecologists have suggested reintroducing them in Denmark, Germany, Italy, Scotland and Wales.

Good or bad?

Not everyone is happy. Ranchers have insisted that they should still be allowed to kill wolves that attack their cattle. "Wolves kill and worry my animals. It affects my income," said one.

Other opponents of wolf reintroduction include elk-hunters, who are staying away. "When we see fewer wolves and more elk, we'll be back," said one.

By 2011, there were 98 wolves in Yellowstone, forming 10 packs. Wolf-watching brings in $35 million a year in tourist spending.

In 1972, scientists showed how much Yellowstone had changed and suggested **reinstating** wolves.

By 2005, wolves were killing more than 1000 elk a year in Yellowstone. The carcasses they left provided more food for ravens, magpies, and bald and golden eagles.

In 1995, 41 wolves were reintroduced to Yellowstone.

Wolves were protected under the Endangered Species Act of 1973.

Was it right to bring the wolves back? Would you like wolves to be reintroduced to the area where you live?

DON'T run!

What would you do if a wild animal attacked? Forget 'running away' or 'dodging it' as most top predators are faster and more agile than you. The best protection is to avoid getting close and make plenty of noise to show where you are, because they don't really want to meet you, either.

Crocodiles have 24 sharp teeth for gripping prey but they can't chew – they bite and swallow victims in chunks.

Near miss

On 21st April 2013, Frenchman Yoann Galeran was swimming in Gove Harbour, Northern Australia, when a crocodile pounced. "It went straight away to the top of my head and, diving under the water, it tried to do that spinning thing," said 29-year-old Galeran, who struggled free, punched the crocodile and swam away. "My head was in the crocodile's mouth for less than a second but it was long enough to give me two puncture wounds on the back of my neck and another three or four punctures on each side of my head."

Attack and defence

	How they attack	What to do
Crocodile or alligator	Bites and grips, then drags its prey into and under the water and rolls it over and over to drown it – the 'death roll'.	Blow a whistle – they don't like the noise. Push the jaws shut.
Shark	Bites to cause deep wounds, then waits for its victim to bleed to death or drown	Scratch or punch the eyes and gills.
Grizzly bear	Stalks prey, then charges, slashing with its claws and biting.	Stand tall and look calm. Speak softly in a deep voice and wave your arms. If it charges, stay still – it's usually a bluff. Curl up and play dead – it may lose interest.
Big cat such as a lion or tiger	Stalks prey until it is within leaping distance. Grips the neck to strangle its victim.	Raise your hands and open out your coat to make yourself look big. Yell and shout and throw sticks and rocks. Hit it on the nose.
Constricting snake such as python or anaconda	Coils round its victim and crushes air out of the body, suffocating its prey.	Keep its coils from your neck and chest. Don't breathe out: the snake will squeeze tighter. Bite its tail or bash it with a rock.

What would you do if you met a top predator?

DID YOU KNOW?

Crocodiles have receptors in their jaw which are sensitive to vibrations in the water. This makes it easier for them to hunt their prey!

World's most dangerous

Which animal kills more than all the tigers, lions, hippos, rhinos and deadly snakes in the world? This powerful creature kills more than 700 000 people every minute, that's more than one a minute! And what is it? A tiny insect called a mosquito.

Mosquitos live everywhere except Antarctica. Females cannot breed without drinking animal blood and some species of mosquito carry **parasites** that cause a **severe** disease called malaria when transmitted to humans.

> **Approximately half of the world's population is at risk of malaria.**
>
> World Health Organization.

The most dangerous animal on the planet

But there is an animal that is potentially even more dangerous than the mosquito – in fact, more dangerous than all the animals in this book; an animal that has the power to bring species to extinction and to cause Earth irreparable damage. And what is this animal? It's ... us.

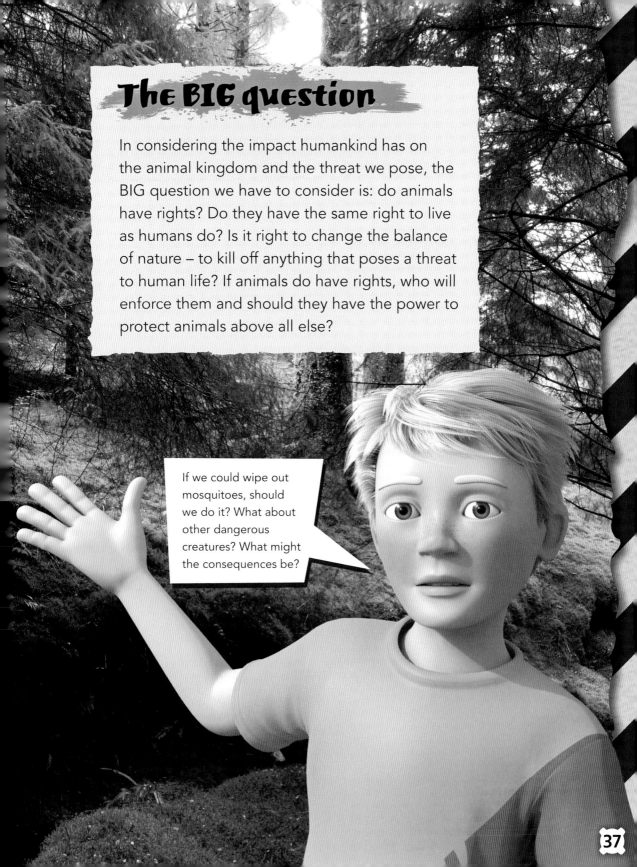

The BIG question

In considering the impact humankind has on the animal kingdom and the threat we pose, the BIG question we have to consider is: do animals have rights? Do they have the same right to live as humans do? Is it right to change the balance of nature – to kill off anything that poses a threat to human life? If animals do have rights, who will enforce them and should they have the power to protect animals above all else?

If we could wipe out mosquitoes, should we do it? What about other dangerous creatures? What might the consequences be?

Future Fears

The human population is growing. At the moment it is 7.2 billion and it is forecast to reach 9.6 billion by 2050. All those people will need homes and food and that means our cities will need to expand and we will have to build extra infrastructure to link them – more roads, railways and airports.

The rising number of mouths to feed will demand that farmers squeeze more food from their land and our desire for new technology will encourage industrial firms to extract more minerals from the ground. None of which is good news for our animal neighbours!

Animals under pressure

Already, environments such as rainforests are under enormous threat from human expansion and the battle has begun to conquer the Arctic for its oil reserves. Animals will have less space and more people will have to live closer to dangerous creatures.

Is the answer to cull them so that they pose no threat? Or reserve land where we preserve their habitats? If so, who will run these?

With the rising population and increasing demand for land, what is the best way to share our planet with deadly creatures?

Glossary

ancestor	a species from which a being is descended
bestiarii	gladiators who used to fight wild animals
constrictor	a snake that kills prey by coiling tightly round it
culling	reducing the population of certain animals by killing them
domesticated	to be tame, kept as a pet
eco-tourism	a type of tourism focussed on appreciation and preservation of the environment
encroach	to move on to the land of another creature
fjord	a stretch of sea bordered by steep cliffs, usually found in Scandinavia
genetic	passed down through genes (**genes** are the building blocks that determine how we look)
mauled	handled roughly (by wild animals)
parasite	an organism that lives on or in another organism
primates	a group of animals that includes human beings, apes, and monkeys
put down	to end an animal's life, usually because it is suffering
reinstate	to put something back as it was before
restrictions	a set of rules or barriers that limit something
scavenge	to take something from something that has been thrown away
severe	serious; harsh
zoochosis	behaviours and problems displayed by animals kept in captivity for a long time

Index